Visual Geography Series®

ENGLAND

...in Pictures

Prepared by
Geography Department

Lerner Publications Company
Minneapolis

Independent Picture Service

**In previous centuries, anyone in danger of capture could
find refuge in England's Durham Cathedral by sounding this
doorknocker on the church's north door.**

This book is an all-new edition in the Visual Geography Series. Previous editions were published by
Sterling Publishing Company, New York City. The
text, set in 10/12 Century Textbook, is fully revised
and updated, and new photographs, maps, charts, and
captions have been added.

LIBRARY OF CONGRESS CATALOGING-IN-PUBLICATION DATA

England in pictures / prepared by Geography Depart-
  ment, Lerner Publications Company.
  p. cm. — (Visual geography series)
  Rev. ed. of: England in pictures / by James Nach.
  Includes bibliographical references.
  Summary: Introduces the topography, history, soci-
ety, economy, and governmental structure of England.
  ISBN 0-8225-1874-0
  1. England. 2. England—Description and travel—
Views. [1. England.] I. Nach, James. England in pic-
tures. II. Lerner Publications Company. Geography
Dept. III. Series: Visual geography series (Minneapolis,
Minn.)
DA27.5.E528   1990   89-78070
942—dc20   CIP
                                 AC

International Standard Book Number: 0-8225-1874-0
Library of Congress Catalog Card Number: 89-78070

VISUAL GEOGRAPHY SERIES®

Publisher
Harry Jonas Lerner
Associate Publisher
Nancy M. Campbell
Senior Editor
Mary M. Rodgers
Editors
Gretchen Bratvold
Dan Filbin
Phyllis Schuster
Photo Researcher
Kerstin Coyle
Editorial/Photo Assistant
Marybeth Campbell
Consultants/Contributors
Barbara Lukermann
Sandra K. Davis
Designer
Jim Simondet
Cartographer
Carol F. Barrett
Indexers
Kristine S. Schubert
Sylvia Timian
Production Manager
Gary J. Hansen

Courtesy of Minneapolis Public Library and Information Center

**Villages and towns throughout England offer tea and cakes
as a light afternoon meal.**

Acknowledgments

Title page photo by Zakhary Bluband.

Elevation contours adapted from *The Times Atlas of
the World*, seventh comprehensive edition (New York:
Times Books, 1985).

1 2 3 4 5 6 7 8 9 10 99 98 97 96 95 94 93 92 91 90

Courtesy of Rugby Advertiser

Lawn bowlers of all ages size up their opponents' position. A game with a long past, lawn bowling—also known as bowls—is played on a flat surface called a green. The object is for one team to roll more of the lopsided black balls close to the jack (the small white ball) than the opposing team does.

Contents

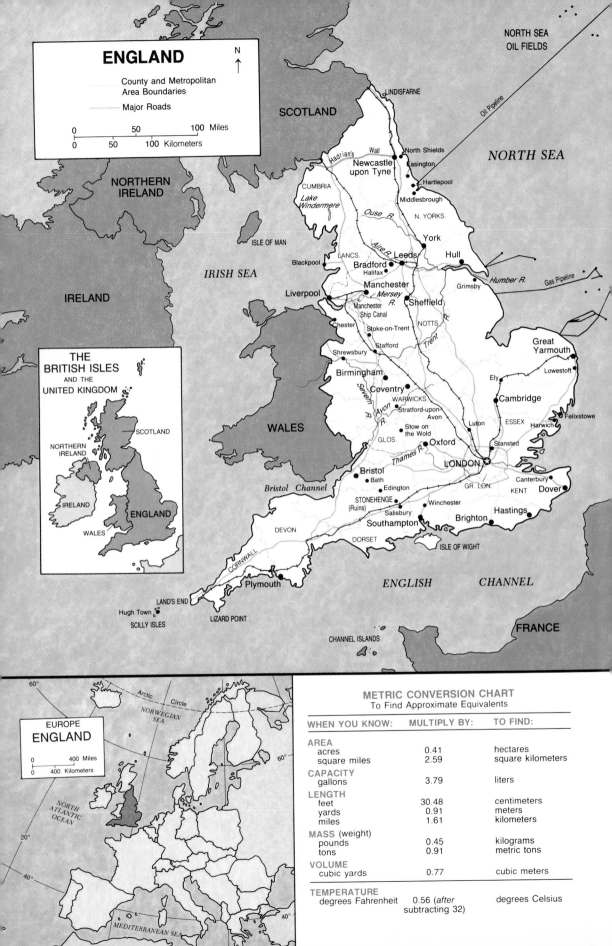

ENGLAND

N ↑

County and Metropolitan
Area Boundaries

Major Roads

0   50   100 Miles
0   50   100 Kilometers

SCOTLAND

NORTHERN
IRELAND

NORTH SEA

LINDISFARNE

Hadrian's   Wall
North Shields
Newcastle   Easington
upon Tyne
Hartlepool
CUMBRIA
Middlesbrough
Lake
Windermere   Ouse R.   N. YORKS.

ISLE OF MAN

LANCS.   Aire R.   York
Blackpool   Leeds   Hull
Bradford
Halifax
Manchester   Grimsby   *Humber R.*   Gas Pipeline
IRISH SEA   *Mersey*
Liverpool   *R.*   Sheffield
Manchester
Ship Canal   NOTTS.
IRELAND   Chester   Stoke-on-Trent
Stafford   *Trent*   Great
Shrewsbury   *R.*   Yarmouth

Birmingham   Lowestoft
Ely
Coventry   Cambridge
Severn   WARWICKS.
R.   Stratford-upon-   ESSEX   Felixstowe
Avon   Avon   Harwich
R.   Stow on   Luton
the Wold   Stansted
GLOS.   Oxford   LONDON
Thames R.   Canterbury
Bristol   GR. LON.   KENT   Dover
WALES   Bath
Bristol Channel   Edington   Hastings
STONEHENGE   Winchester
(Ruins)   Brighton
Salisbury
Southampton
DEVON
DORSET   ISLE OF WIGHT

ENGLISH   CHANNEL

CORNWALL   FRANCE
Plymouth
LAND'S END
Hugh Town
SCILLY ISLES   LIZARD POINT

CHANNEL ISLANDS

NORTH SEA
OIL FIELDS

Oil Pipeline

THE
BRITISH ISLES
AND THE
UNITED KINGDOM

SCOTLAND

NORTHERN
IRELAND

IRELAND   ENGLAND

WALES

EUROPE
ENGLAND

0   400 Miles
0   400 Kilometers

60°
Arctic   Circle
NORWEGIAN
SEA
60°
NORTH
ATLANTIC
OCEAN
20°
40°
40°
MEDITERRANEAN SEA
20°

METRIC CONVERSION CHART
To Find Approximate Equivalents

WHEN YOU KNOW:	MULTIPLY BY:	TO FIND:
AREA		
acres	0.41	hectares
square miles	2.59	square kilometers
CAPACITY		
gallons	3.79	liters
LENGTH		
feet	30.48	centimeters
yards	0.91	meters
miles	1.61	kilometers
MASS (weight)		
pounds	0.45	kilograms
tons	0.91	metric tons
VOLUME		
cubic yards	0.77	cubic meters
TEMPERATURE		
degrees Fahrenheit	0.56 (*after* subtracting 32)	degrees Celsius

Workers positioned at well-spaced intervals assemble cars at an automotive factory in Essex, eastern England. Transportation equipment is one of the country's main manufactured items.

Introduction

England is the largest country within a European nation called the United Kingdom of Great Britain and Northern Ireland. England, Scotland, and Wales form Great Britain. Northern Ireland covers the northeastern section of the island of Ireland, which lies west of Great Britain. A unified nation since 1707, the United Kingdom has an eventful history. Each of its four countries can also claim a long and colorful past.

Between about 500 B.C. and A.D. 1066, England experienced periodic invasions. During that time, Celts, Romans, Anglo-Saxons, Danes, and Normans crossed the lowlands of England on missions of conquest. These groups brought traditions of law, royal government, literature, and language that have survived to the present day.

England's location and wealth of ports made trade a natural livelihood. By the 1850s, the country had become the hub of a commercial empire that touched six continents. A century later, two world wars and international competition had taken away some of England's markets.

As it had throughout its history, the country adapted, switching its industries from iron to electronics and from cloth to plastics. England also became part of the

European Community (EC)—an association of Western European nations that pursues economic policies of mutual benefit. If current EC plans for commercial unity remain on target, by 1992 England will be part of a powerful trading bloc.

Despite this development, some aspects of England's future remain uncertain. An economic rift is growing between southern England, which prospered in the 1980s, and northern England, which declined. Unemployment is higher in northern England in 1990 than it was in 1980, and inflation is rising. These various economic trends cast a shadow over England's future. Yet the country's people bring a heritage of cooperation and determination to modern challenges. These qualities suggest that England's age-old traditions will survive and that the country will flourish in the coming decades.

Deck chairs line the seashore at Brighton, a popular resort city in southern England.

At the Royal Shakespeare Theatre in Stratford-upon-Avon, two actresses perform a scene from the Shakespearean comedy *As You Like It.* England has a strong theater tradition and has produced many fine actors and playwrights.

Courtesy of British Tourist Authority

A lone walker makes her way toward the Bedruthan Steps—rock formations on the jagged coast of Cornwall in southwestern England. The pressure of too many visitors on this stretch of coastline has caused soil erosion and other environmental damage. As a result, a government agency carefully maintains the pathways and beaches.

1) The Land

Located just northwest of mainland Europe, the island of Great Britain is made up of three parts. Scotland is in the north, Wales lies in the west, and England covers the southern and largest portion. Great Britain is part of the British Isles, a group of islands that also includes Ireland, the Channel Islands, and the Isles of Wight, of Scilly, and of Man. The Isle of Wight and the Scilly Isles come under England's administrative authority.

With a total area of 50,333 square miles, England is slightly bigger than the state of New York. The Cheviot Hills divide En-

gland and Scotland. Wales, the Irish Sea, and the Atlantic Ocean lie along England's western border. The North Sea touches the country's eastern coast, and the English Channel separates southern England from France.

Topography

Roughly triangular in shape, England has a long, irregular coastline, and none of its land lies more than 75 miles from the sea. The country's main topographical features are the rugged highlands of the north and southwest and the low-lying plains and valleys of the center and southeast.

NORTHERN AND SOUTHWESTERN UPLANDS

Often called the backbone of England, the Pennine Chain is a series of uplands that runs through northern England in a north-south direction. The generally flat-topped, worn-down chain stretches from the Scottish border to the center of the country—a section called the Midlands. Fertile plains lie on either side of the Pennines, whose highest point is Cross Fell (2,930 feet). Other highlands in the north are the Yorkshire Moors and the Cumbrian Mountains.

West of the Pennines and in the Cumbrian Mountains is the Lake District—a scenic region of lakes and peaks. The area contains Scafell Pike (3,210 feet), England's highest point, and Lake Windermere, the country's largest inland body of water.

Photo by Kay Shaw Photography

Rolling farmland, studded with round bales of hay, stretches to the horizon near Stow on the Wold in Gloucestershire.

Courtesy of LeeAnne Engfer

Within the Peak District—a protected area at the southern end of the Pennine Chain—a fly-fisherman casts his line in a narrow stream.

The southwestern peninsula has a different landscape from that of northern England, although both areas contain rugged uplands. Beginning south of the Bristol Channel, the peninsula includes Land's End —England's westernmost spot—and Lizard Point, the country's southernmost location.

Southwestern England's dominant features are the broad moorlands at Exmoor and Dartmoor. These open expanses of land are covered with grasses and low shrubs on old, weathered granite formations. At some places along the coast, the land drops steeply to the sea, creating towering cliffs.

CENTRAL AND SOUTHEASTERN LOWLANDS

Situated at the southern end of the Pennines, the Midlands begin a region of rolling hills and green valleys that covers the rest of the country. Most of England's people live in these lowland areas, where many farms and important industries are located. Although part of a grassy plain, the Midlands are famous for the manufacturing facilities in and around the city of Birmingham.

To the east, along the coast of the North Sea, lies some of England's richest farmland. Called the Fens, this low-lying region was once a huge marsh (*fen* is an English word for marsh) but has been drained and cultivated for centuries. The lowest point in England—at Ely—is in the Fens and can measure 15 feet below sea level when the North Sea is at high tide.

South of the Thames River, which runs through the capital city of London, is a series of low, chalk hills and grass-covered valleys known as downs. At certain points, the downs abruptly meet the sea, creating dramatically steep cliffs. Because the underlying soil is chalky, some cliffs—such as those at Dover—look white. The White Cliffs of Dover are a famous landmark for travelers who arrive from the European mainland by boat.

The lower part of Tower Bridge is raised to allow a vessel to travel up the Thames River in London, England's capital city. From the bridge's upper section, viewers can watch the river's traffic.

Rivers

Although England contains many rivers, none of them is very long. The waterways flow from upland areas to the seas that surround the British Isles. At some estuaries—outlets where the rivers meet the seas—fine harbors exist. They include the ports of London, Liverpool, Bristol, and Hull.

With a 215-mile course, the Thames is the longest river completely within England's boundaries. Beginning in the Cotswold Hills of western England, the Thames winds through the southern part of the country. At London, the river broadens into an estuary, and docks line its banks farther downstream. As the Thames flows through the heart of the capital, it passes under many bridges and eventually meets the North Sea.

Canals connect many of England's rivers, creating long water routes. Some of the shorter canals have become popular as waterways for pleasure cruises.

In the 1960s, when London's fog was a famous feature of life in the capital, a London policeman—called a bobby—could walk his beat engulfed in mist. Since then, however, scientists have found that the fog resulted from air pollution, which strict regulations have nearly eliminated.

Independent Picture Service

Slightly longer than the Thames is the Severn River, which travels through both England and Wales. Originating in central Wales, the waterway curves eastward into England near Shrewsbury. The Severn then turns southward to empty into the Bristol Channel, an arm of the Atlantic Ocean. Canals connect the Severn with the Thames, the Trent, and the Mersey rivers.

The Trent, England's third longest river, begins in the center of the country. Flowing eastward, the waterway joins the Ouse River to form the Humber, an estuary where the North Sea port of Hull is located. The Mersey River rises in northwestern England. Extended by canal to Manchester, the Mersey's short course brings it to a broad estuary at Liverpool on the Irish Sea.

Climate

The North Atlantic Current—a branch of the warm, Caribbean-based Gulf Stream Current—raises the temperature of the waters that surround England. Winds that pass over the North Atlantic Current arrive in southwestern England as warm gusts, moderating the country's temperatures. Since England is small in size, the winds remain warm as they pass over the land. These factors contribute to England's mild climate, particularly along the southwestern coast.

In winter, cold air from the European continent pushes its way westward across the North Sea and gives northeastern England below-freezing temperatures. In the southeast, on the other hand, London's January temperatures, usually stay at about 40° F. Southeastern England has hotter summers than the southwest and the north. In July, London's average temperature is 63° F.

Because western and highland areas of England are exposed to moisture-laden winds, these regions receive the greatest amount of rainfall—in some years, as much as 100 inches. Parts of the Lake District get over 60 inches of precipitation each year. Average annual rainfall in the southeast is less than 25 inches. Although October is generally the wettest month for most of England, precipitation occurs throughout the year. Rain often arrives as a mist or steady drizzle, rather than as a downpour.

Once famous for its thick fog, London has rarely experienced this form of weather since 1980. Studies showed that the fog was the result of pollution from cars and factories that burned gas and coal. Recent laws have helped to reduce air pollution in the capital and other large cities, particularly by banning the use of high-sulfur coal for domestic heating.

11

In summer, the purple blossoms of heather—a low, evergreen shrub—cover the moors (open wilderness) of northeastern England. Livestock often graze on young heather plants.

Flora and Fauna

At one time, Great Britain was covered with trees. About 30 percent of the island is forested in the modern era. Centuries of clearing land for housing and farming have left few sizable forests in England, which has only 7 percent of the island's woodlands. Large, private estates contain some of the best-preserved natural vegetation.

Oak, beech, and other hardwoods are the dominant trees in English forests, although yew trees thrive in the chalky soil of the southeast.

Human activities have had little effect on the moors, whose short, scrubby vegetation includes gorse (a yellowish plant) and heather. The blossoms of this low, evergreen shrub give the moors a purplish

A mute swan swims in a pond in southwestern England. Less noisy than other swan species, mute swans make hissing sounds when angry. Historically, English monarchs prized these animals as valuable pets and food sources. To mark royal ownership, some mute swans were branded on their beaks—a custom that continues in London. Each year, members of two ancient trade guilds—the Dyers' Company and the Vintners' Company—brand swans as the property of Queen Elizabeth II. She can also claim ownership of any unmarked swan that lives on the Thames.

hue in summer. To preserve the English countryside, the government has set aside large areas for national parks and protected habitats.

Hunters have eliminated many of the country's animals. Some of the species that have survived—such as fox, partridge, and grouse—are bred to provide sport for wealthy people. Although few large mammals live in England, smaller animals include badgers, weasels, and rabbits. English bird-watchers keep track of several hundred species of birds, such as pipits, sparrows, mute swans, and wrens, which either migrate to England during part of the year or live there permanently.

Among aquatic species, freshwater trout and salmon attract many fishing enthusiasts to local rivers. Some English people make their living catching herring, cod, mackerel, and other saltwater fish that abound in the waters around the British Isles.

Natural Resources

Miners have worked England's mineral deposits since ancient times, and some supplies—such as those of tin and lead—have largely been exhausted. Nevertheless, the country contains significant reserves of oil, natural gas, and coal.

Discoveries of natural gas in the 1960s and of oil in the 1970s brought much-needed income to the United Kingdom. Both gas and oil lie in the North Sea, and small oil fields exist in central England. The country's coal reserves run in broad seams through northern and central England.

Courtesy of British Coal Corporation

Although the number of coal mines has declined, England still contains significant reserves of the mineral. Here, a worker guides a piece of heavy equipment as it cuts through the coalface and deposits the coal chunks on a conveyor belt.

London

London, the capital of both Britain and England, is located in the southeast. The city and its surrounding communities—together called Greater London—have more than 6.7 million residents.

Inhabited for over 2,000 years, London has a long history. The capital was once a Roman city (called Londinium) and was an active trading hub during the Middle Ages (from the fifth to the fourteenth centuries). The center of the modern metropolis is the City of London, where the Romans settled in the first century A.D. This same area now contains many of Britain's financial institutions. Standing beside the modern office buildings in the City of London are historic structures, such as St. Paul's Cathedral and the Bank of England.

Among London's most famous buildings is the Tower of London. Constructed as a stronghold in the late eleventh century, the riverside fort served as a prison, a residence, and a weapons depot. For centuries, the tower has contained the crown jewels—the gems, crowns, swords, and other finery that the royal family uses on state occasions.

Travelers emerge from Leicester Square Station, part of London's underground transportation system. Commonly called "the tube," the network of train tracks carries many of the capital's residents and visitors to jobs, shops, and theaters.

Also within central London are governmental centers, such as the Houses of Parliament, and shopping and entertainment districts. In recent years, developers have transformed much of London's dockyards—once the setting of the city's vast commercial activities—into printing plants, shops, restaurants, offices, and expensive housing. Beyond these well-known areas are lively and historic sections that add to Greater London's variety. They extend across some of London's boroughs (local governmental units), which once were outlying villages.

Surrounding the metropolis is the "Green Belt"—a band of countryside meant to limit the city's growth. Housing authorities have moved low-income families from the slums that encircle central London to new towns beyond the Green Belt. Nevertheless, London has the usual disadvantages of most urban areas—crowded conditions, crime, and poverty. Many boroughs have experienced violence among the minority groups living there.

Courtesy of European Travel Commission

At Buckingham Palace, the queen's London residence, members of the Guards Division end the ceremony known as the changing of the guard. This daily parade involves the replacement of one group of royal guards with its relief shift from a nearby barracks. Once on duty, the guards — wearing bright red coats and heavy, bearskin caps — slowly march in front of the entrance of the palace.

15

Cars curve around the Bull Ring—a street leading to the downtown area of Birmingham, England's second largest city.

Secondary Urban Centers

Although London is England's biggest city, the country has other large population centers. These places owe their rapid growth to the nineteenth-century Industrial Revolution, which expanded factories and created jobs in urban areas.

Birmingham (population 2.6 million) contained industries as early as the 1100s. The nearby wealth of coal and iron-ore deposits made the city an important manufacturing hub in the 1800s. Birmingham's natural resources attracted industry to the area, and the city's population rose dramatically. Heavily bombed in World War II (1939–1945), Birmingham has since been rebuilt and expanded. Its main industries produce cars, electronic equipment, and tools.

Manchester (population 2.5 million) became a key manufacturer of cotton and textiles in the 1800s. The Manchester Ship Canal connects the city to the Mersey River, providing port facilities for large cargo vessels. Manchester also has an active financial district, an international airport, and excellent railway connections to other large cities in Britain. The city's leading industries make chemicals, cloth, computers, food, tools, and electronic equipment.

Courtesy of Gordon L. Levine

The buildings on Portland Street in Manchester display mixed architectural styles, reflecting the city's growth and change in the last two centuries.

Located in the middle of England's wool-producing area, Leeds (population two million) furnishes much of the country's woolen and synthetic textiles. The city lies in north central England along the Aire River, which is linked by canal to Liverpool. Although established as a wool hub in the 1300s, Leeds has also become a major engineering, cultural, and educational center for northern England. The University of Leeds is one of the country's largest institutions of higher learning.

West of Manchester stands Liverpool (population 1.4 million), England's main port on the Irish Sea. Since World War II, when its docks were severely damaged, Liverpool has declined. It has high unemployment, its port facilities are run down, and much of its nineteenth-century housing is inadequate. Nevertheless, the city still relies on its docks for income. It

Courtesy of British Tourist Authority

Along the waterfront in Liverpool—once northwestern England's thriving port—nineteenth-century structures house the customs and dock offices.

17

also contains car-assembly plants, flour mills, and sugar refineries. In the 1960s, Liverpool became famous as the home of the Beatles, a rock band that revolutionized popular music.

HISTORIC SITES

England abounds with historic smaller cities, towns, and villages. Modern architecture and technology have changed the appearance of large urban centers. Some of England's less populated settlements—such as York and Bath—retain evidence of former times.

Founded as a Roman town called Eboracum, York was an important religious, administrative, and trading hub in northern England in the Middle Ages. The city maintains three ancient gates of entry and is enclosed on three sides by a fourteenth-century wall. Within York's walls stand one of England's largest cathedrals—York Minster—and many narrow streets, including the Shambles.

Warm mineral waters, Roman ruins, and eighteenth-century architecture are found in Bath—a city in southwestern England on the Avon River. Bath still contains parts of a Roman spa built during the period of Roman occupation. In the 1700s, wealthy Europeans began to frequent Bath for its health-giving waters, estab-

Courtesy of Richard Rodgers

The central tower of York Minster—a large cathedral in the northern city of York—rises from behind the trees. Begun in 1220, the church was completed in 1472 and exhibits many types of architectural styles. Fires damaged the minster in 1829, 1840, and 1984.

lishing the Assembly and Pump rooms as trendy gathering places. Sections of the city, such as the Royal Crescent, were designed in the elegant architectural style of the eighteenth century.

Courtesy of Joanne Rodgers

A preference for simplicity and symmetry inspired the builders of the Royal Crescent—a curved street of houses in Bath.

Courtesy of Susan Graves

Many archaeologists have studied the rocks at Stonehenge—a circular site that dates from about 2000 B.C. Scientists suggest that ancient peoples arranged the stones to observe the movement of the sun and moon as well as to enhance their religious rituals.

2) History and Government

England has long perceived itself as distinct from Europe. Yet 40,000 years ago, a land bridge joined the British Isles to the mainland. By 5000 B.C., the last Ice Age had ended, and water from melting ice had submerged the land bridge. Great Britain thus became an island separated from Europe by a narrow channel.

The island's early inhabitants, however, originated on the mainland. They used tools and weapons of stone and bone and cleared the thick native forests for farmland. Additional migrations of Europeans began in about 3000 B.C., with a large group arriving from what is now West Germany in about 2000 B.C.

The Germanic newcomers made their tools of bronze and established circular religious sites—called henges—built of stone or wood. One of these places, named Stonehenge, still stands near the city of Salisbury in south central England.

About 1,500 years later, another migration to England occurred. The new arrivals, known as Celts, originated in northern Europe. A warlike people, the Celts soon conquered the country with their superior iron weapons. They grouped themselves into clans, which fought one another for power. Once settled, the Celts relied on farming to feed themselves. Between 500 and 100 B.C., they transformed England into an agricultural country farmed by many Celtic-speaking groups.

The Roman Era

Isolated by water, England—unlike mainland Europe—had not yet felt the force of the Roman Empire, which was centered in Italy. In 55 B.C., however, Julius Caesar, an important Roman military commander, crossed the English Channel and staged a brief raid on southeastern England. The next year, he came back with a larger army and defeated the strongest Celtic resisters. While the Roman commander was dictating peace terms, Celtic groups revolted in nearby France. The rebellions forced Caesar to leave England without setting up a Roman administration.

In A.D. 43, the Roman emperor Claudius ordered his army to invade England. The Romans landed in the southeast, and the Celts—led by Queen Boudicca—again tried to defend themselves. Despite the efforts of Celtic troops, the Romans had conquered the island by the end of the first century A.D. They named this new province Britannia after a Celtic clan called Brythons.

The conquerors laid roads, built forts, and founded cities. In the A.D. 120s, engineers under the orders of Emperor Hadrian constructed a barrier—called Hadrian's Wall—to keep out the far northern peoples, whom the Romans had failed to subdue. Words from Latin (the language spoken by the Romans) found their way into Celtic dialects. By the third century, Roman missionaries had brought Christianity to the island.

Despite its strong cultural influence, the Roman Empire began to break up in the fourth century. Skilled military commanders and high-ranking nobles competed for power, and Rome's control of its far-flung holdings weakened. Units of the Roman army left Britannia to protect other parts of the empire. By the late fourth century, Germanic peoples had begun to strike at the frontiers of the province without

Photo by Mansell Collection

Riding in a chariot, Queen Boudicca rallied her Celtic troops to fight against the Roman army in about A.D. 60. The queen's efforts failed, and she took poison rather than surrender to her enemies.

Courtesy of Theresa Early

The Romans built baths to take advantage of England's warm, underground mineral springs. The city of Bath became a Roman resort, whose remaining structures modern visitors are still able to view.

In about A.D. 600, Augustine, a missionary of the Roman Catholic Church, baptized the Anglo-Saxon king Aethelberht *(kneeling)*. The Anglo-Saxons had taken control of England in the late 500s.

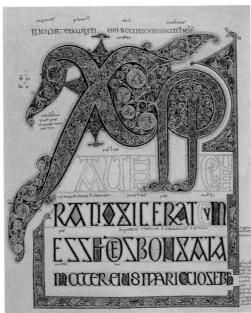

This page from the Lindisfarne Gospels begins the writings of the apostle Matthew. Copied, drawn, and painted by hand in about 700, the Lindisfarne Gospels combine the designs of the Celts, the Anglo-Saxons, and the Catholic church.

meeting much Roman resistance. By the mid-fifth century, the Romans had abandoned their defense of Britannia.

The Arrival of Anglo-Saxons

After the Romans left, various Germanic groups—notably the Angles and the Saxons—began invading the British Isles in warships. Their activities and the revival of Celtic ways wiped out much of the Roman culture in Britannia.

Adding to the turmoil of the Anglo-Saxon invasions was the outbreak of a plague (a deadly disease) in the mid-sixth century. The disease killed many Celts, allowing the Germanic peoples to seize authority. The remaining Celts fled to what are now Wales and the western counties of Cumbria and Cornwall. By the late sixth century, seven separate Anglo-Saxon kingdoms had arisen, namely Kent, Northumbria, East Anglia, Mercia, Wessex, Sussex, and Essex.

In 597, after the Anglo-Saxons took over England, missionaries arrived from Rome, the center of the Catholic Church, to convert the conquerors to Christianity. The head of the expedition, a monk named Augustine, landed in Kent. He baptized its ruler, King Aethelberht, as well as many Kentish citizens.

Aethelberht granted Augustine some land at Canterbury, which soon became the place from which Roman Catholicism spread in England. In time, the other Anglo-Saxon kings also accepted the Christian faith.

The blending of Roman Catholic and Anglo-Saxon art forms reached its height in Northumbria. In monasteries such as Lindisfarne, monks produced beautiful hand-painted manuscripts and scholarly works in Latin—the language of the Church.

MERCIA, WESSEX, AND THE VIKINGS

By the eighth century, large Christian kingdoms had replaced the Anglo-Saxon realms of previous periods. Under its ruler

Offa, the kingdom of Mercia—which was in west central England—exercised authority from 757 to 796. Along the Welsh border, Offa built a long, high embankment, called Offa's Dyke, that defined the western boundary of his realm. Weak kings succeeded Offa, and by the ninth century, Wessex—which lay in central and southwestern England—was the strongest English kingdom.

Roughly at this same time, adventurers called Vikings used their superior seafaring and war-making skills to attack England. The fighters came from Scandinavia, a region that includes Norway, Denmark, and Sweden. The non-Christian Vikings sacked Lindisfarne in 793 and raided Wessex on a separate expedition in the 790s.

After several decades of piracy, Danish Vikings sought to conquer England so they could settle and trade in the area. To achieve their goal, the Danes attacked Wessex. In the spring of 878, King Alfred of Wessex and his fighters defeated the Danish army under King Guthrum at Edington. By 886 Alfred and Guthrum had agreed on the boundaries between their two kingdoms. The Danish lands, called the Danelaw, included most of northern and eastern England.

Danish and Norman Conquests

Alfred's successors inherited a unified and peaceful kingdom. The peace lasted until the early eleventh century, when a second wave of Danish invasions occurred. To hold off the new Viking conquerors, King Aethelred of Wessex collected a tax—called Danegeld—to bribe the Vikings not to attack. This tactic worked for a while, until the Danes came with a large force in 1013.

Under their king Sweyn, the Danish Vikings conquered Aethelred's realm. After Sweyn's death in 1014, his kingdom passed to his son Canute, who gained the support of both the English and the Danes. Ca-

Courtesy of Wayland (Publishers) Limited

A statue of King Alfred the Great stands in Winchester, the ancient capital of Wessex (Alfred's ninth-century realm in southwestern England). After defeating Danish raiders called Vikings, Alfred set about improving his kingdom, which eventually included most of England. He fortified towns and reorganized them into administrative units. An educated man, the king encouraged learning and the arts, bringing teachers and craftspeople to Wessex. A ninth-century book—called *The Anglo-Saxon Chronicle*—details Alfred's efforts to unify and strengthen the kingdom.

nute's successors, however, were not as popular. In addition, they died without heirs.

In 1042 the leaders of Wessex chose Aethelred's son Edward, who had grown up in Normandy (now part of France), to be king of England. A deeply religious monarch, King Edward, who is called "the Confessor," spent much of his reign completing a fine church in London where Westminster Abbey now stands.

When Edward died without an heir in 1066, English leaders named his brother-in-law Harold to succeed him. Harold knew his hold on the throne was not secure because there were other people who had strong claims to the kingship. One of them was William of Normandy, a distant relative of Edward. William and his army landed in southern England and defeated Harold on October 14, 1066, at the Battle of Hastings. Thereafter known as William the Conqueror, William became the first Norman king of England.

CHANGES UNDER THE NORMANS

After the Norman victory, large numbers of Norman nobles, church officials, clerks, artisans, and merchants arrived in England. William the Conqueror took away lands from the English and gave the holdings to Normans. The Normans introduced their own building styles, which in time appeared in new castles and cathedrals.

French, which all Normans spoke, became the language of wealthy and educated people. Most people below the highest levels of society still used an early form of English, which had evolved from the Anglo-Saxon language.

The Norman Conquest also dramatically changed the power structure in England, making landowners—no matter how rich —secondary to the king. Except for the monarch, everyone was responsible to another, higher-ranking person. William and his heirs strengthened this system—called feudalism—over the next century.

Feudalism survived despite civil wars and isolated rebellions of dissatisfied Norman and English nobles. By 1154 the Norman style of government was strongly established. In that year, William's great-grandson Henry of Anjou inherited the English throne and added it to his family's

One of many panels from the Bayeux Tapestry (an embroidered wall hanging) shows King Harold on the English throne. His defeat by William of Normandy in 1066 brought to power the French-speaking Norman kings of England. French artisans produced the long tapestry soon after William's victory, possibly to confirm his right to the English crown. The cloth depicts the events of the Norman Conquest along with everyday scenes of eleventh-century life.

Independent Picture Service

large holdings of Anjou, Aquitaine, and Normandy in France.

The Plantagenets

As Henry II, Henry of Anjou was the first king of the Angevin dynasty (family of rulers). The Angevin emblem was a small flower called *plante genêt* in French, and the dynasty's members often carried the last name Plantagenet.

Because the Plantagenet kings held land in both England and France, trade with Europe expanded greatly. English breeds of sheep produced fine grades of wool for export, and in time England became known on the continent for its woolen cloth.

Most English people lived and worked on the farming estates of wealthy nobles. Because they did not own land, these laborers, called serfs, were virtual slaves and seldom were able to free themselves of their service to landowners. Craftspeople and traders had more personal liberty, but the strict rules of their professions often dictated where and how they worked.

Although the Plantagenet kings brought some stability to England, their reigns were not without conflicts. Henry II quarreled with the Church over legal reforms that he was trying to make. England's archbishop of Canterbury, Thomas Becket, fought for the Church's rights—a stance that cost him his life. Becket was

Photo by Bettmann Archive

In 1215 nobles and religious officials gathered around King John as he signed the *Magna Carta* (Great Charter). It confirmed their rights and put limitations on royal power.

Independent Picture Service

Charters and other important documents were made legally binding through the use of royal seals, such as this one that belonged to John's son Henry III. Around the rim are the Latin words, "Henry by the Grace of God King of England, Lord of Ireland, Duke of Aquitaine."

An old manuscript page shows two English wool dyers at work. Established by the Romans, the wool industry remained a vital part of England's economy for many centuries. Woolen fabric became an important export for the country.

murdered in Canterbury Cathedral in 1170. Henry II did penance in public for having caused the archbishop's death.

Henry II's son John struggled against many high-ranking nobles (collectively called barons), who felt that he was not running the country fairly or efficiently. The outcome of their dispute was the *Magna Carta* (Great Charter), which the barons forced John to sign in 1215. This document, which has become a cornerstone of English law, outlined rights that the barons believed were important for good government. The rights included protection against unlawful taxes and the freedom of the Church from royal influence.

When John's son, Henry III, also quarreled with the barons, some of them—led by Simon de Montfort—rebelled. Their victories forced the king to accept limits to his power. As a result, for a short time, Henry III ruled with the advice of an appointed parliament, whose members came from the nobility and the large towns. His successor, Edward I, regularly asked Parliament for its advice in running the kingdom.

PLANTAGENET WARS

Edward I and later Plantagenet kings needed the financial support of Parliament to wage wars against Wales, Scotland, and France. Edward I subdued Wales in 1282 and claimed all of the Welsh lands, building a string of castles to defend them. His successor, Edward II, was a weak king who lost a major battle against the Scots at Bannockburn in 1314. The defeat helped Scotland to remain independent of England for nearly 400 years.

English troops under Edward III won battles against larger French forces during the Hundred Years' War (1337–1453). The prolonged fighting drained treasuries and decreased populations on both sides, driving English workers to revolt in 1381. Led by Wat Tyler, the rebels objected to the heavy taxes that Edward III's grandson, Richard II, collected to fund the long war. Richard's policies caused Parliament to depose him in 1399.

25

Civil wars began to ravage the country in the 1400s, as two branches of the Plantagenet family—the Lancastrians and the Yorkists—fought for control of the monarchy. Historians call these conflicts the Wars of the Roses because the emblem for the House of Lancaster was a red rose and the badge for the House of York was a white rose.

After deposing Richard II, Parliament chose Henry of Lancaster to be king. As Henry IV, he spent his reign trying to protect the kingdom from Yorkist rebellions. The bloodiest battles of the Wars of the Roses began in 1455, under Henry IV's grandson, the feeble-minded Henry VI. The Yorkist Edward IV seized the monarchy in 1461 and, except for a short interruption, held on to the throne until his death in 1483.

Independent Picture Service

Made up of rich nobles, landowners, and merchants, the first parliaments often provided money for wars and other foreign ventures. In 1399 Parliament was powerful enough to remove King Richard II from the throne.

In 1485 a minor Lancastrian claimant named Henry Tudor defeated the last Yorkist ruler in the Battle of Bosworth. Because of the Tudor victory, Parliament confirmed Henry as king. To mend the long rift between the two Plantagenet houses, Henry VII married Elizabeth of York, the daughter of Edward IV. Together, they founded the Tudor dynasty.

The Tudors

The realm over which Henry VII reigned had changed a great deal since the Norman Conquest of 1066. Little distinction remained between Normans and Anglo-Saxons, because centuries of intermarriage had mixed the two groups. Although outbreaks of the bubonic plague in the 1300s had dramatically decreased England's population, by the late 1400s the number of people was rising again.

Goods from all over Europe found their way to London, the capital city. English sheep, which numbered in the millions, supplied the wool trade and a growing cloth industry. The centers of cloth production—Leeds, Halifax, and Bradford—became more prosperous than cities that exported raw wool.

A thrifty and clever man, Henry VII strengthened the monarchy and improved England's financial position. In 1509 he left a rich and stable kingdom to his successor, Henry VIII. The new king established a strong navy, fought wars against France, and formally united England and Wales. Henry's religious writings earned him the approval of the Roman Catholic pope. These works appeared when many Europeans were rejecting the authority of the Church—a movement called the Protestant Reformation.

At that time, most people would only accept a male as heir to the English kingdom. Although Henry had a daughter, he and his Spanish wife had no living sons. Henry VIII asked the pope to dissolve his marriage so the king could marry someone else. The pope's refusal to allow a divorce caused Henry to declare himself head of the church in England in 1534. The kingdom broke its ties to the Roman Catholic Church and joined the Protestant Reformation that was sweeping Europe.

THE ELIZABETHAN AGE

By the time of his death in 1547, Henry VIII had married six times. All three of his children ruled after him. Despite the prejudice against her gender, Henry's last surviving child—his daughter, Elizabeth —came to the throne in 1558 at the age of 25. She transformed England from a small seafaring nation into a great naval power. A Protestant, Elizabeth confirmed the Church of England as the country's official religious organization. She also chose her ministers well and worked skillfully with the Parliaments that served during her 45-year reign.

By the mid-sixteenth century, Parliament had changed from an advisory council to an essential element of royal government. This legislative body, consisting of the House of Lords and the House of Commons, imposed taxes and wrote laws. The House of Lords was made up of nobles and high officials of the Church of England. Members of the Commons were from the gentry—important landowners and merchants who were just below the nobility in social status.

Elizabeth's father had laid the foundation of a strong navy. When Spain—a rival European power—attempted to invade England by sea in 1588, the English navy was ready. The Spanish Armada (fleet of ships) met stiff English resistance and escaped with only half of its 130 vessels still afloat. This naval victory established England as a strong European power.

The Stuarts

An unmarried queen, Elizabeth left no direct heir. Her crown passed to King James VI of Scotland, who was descended

Independent Picture Service

The Tudor dynasty (family of rulers) ruled from 1485 to 1603. Its last and perhaps greatest member was Elizabeth I *(pictured)*. During her reign, England developed a strong navy, explored uncharted areas of the world, and extended its trading contacts. Literature flourished, bringing the works of Shakespeare, Edmund Spenser, and Christopher Marlowe to public attention.

from one of Henry VIII's sisters. In 1603— as James I—he became the first English monarch of the royal House of Stuart. He combined the English and Scottish realms in a personal union but ruled them as separate kingdoms.

James's style of governing differed from the standard English practice. He wanted to rule absolutely and ignored the advice of Parliament. The king's limited acceptance of Parliament and that body's unwillingness to give up power planted the seeds of civil war. When James I died in 1625, his son, Charles I, inherited this conflict. The new king quarreled with Parliament over money and dismissed and recalled the legislature at will. By the 1640s, many members of Parliament and some important merchants wanted to change the situation.

Independent Picture Service

Elizabeth's successors fought with Parliament more than they cooperated with it. By the 1640s, frustrated parliamentary members such as Oliver Cromwell *(above)* favored civil war. Victories by Cromwell's forces allowed him to abolish the monarchy and to head a new government.

Civil war broke out in 1642 and pitted the Royalists, who supported the king, against the Parliamentarians, who backed Parliament. Under their commander Oliver Cromwell, the parliamentary forces won victories at Marston Moor in 1644 and at Naseby in 1645. By 1647 Charles I was in the hands of the Parliamentarians, and his eldest son had fled to the European mainland. After a public trial, Charles I was beheaded in 1649.

Cromwell's victories and Charles I's execution established Parliament's rule over the country. For more than a decade, England was a republic, not a monarchy. Cromwell, who followed a strict Protestant sect known as Puritanism, headed the government and imposed many of his Puritan ideas. His excellent military skill won him political power, but he used his authority to censor the press, to tax illegally, and to establish his religious views. These policies doomed his efforts to set up a permanent

republic. Cromwell died in 1658, and by 1660 a new Parliament had placed Charles I's son, Charles II, on the throne.

PARLIAMENT AND THE MONARCHY

The restoration of the monarchy occurred because both Parliament and the king were willing to work together. Charles II understood and accepted his role, and Parliament retained most of the powers it had won in the previous decade. During Charles II's reign, the first English political parties formed. The Tories generally supported the authority of the monarch and the Church of England. The Whigs favored policies that benefited trade and that expanded parliamentary power.

Protestant-Catholic tensions, which had been present during Charles II's reign, became severe when his Catholic brother, James, inherited the throne in 1685. By

Photo by National Portrait Gallery, London

Cromwell's efforts to remake England failed, and Parliament offered the crown to Charles II. Clear about his royal role, the new king encouraged artistic, scientific, and literary achievements.

1689 Parliament had offered the crown to James II's Protestant daughter Mary and her husband, William, who also had a strong claim to the English throne. James II fled the country, and William and Mary reigned jointly. They accepted the Bill of Rights—a document that ensured freedom of speech and fair trials and that broadened the powers of Parliament. This assembly now ruled England, although the monarch retained some authority.

Under Mary's younger sister, Anne—the last of the Stuart monarchs—England's military supremacy grew as the country waged successful wars against France and Spain. These victories enlarged England's colonial holdings in Asia, Africa, and North America. In 1707 Anne signed the Act of Union, which formally combined England, Wales, and Scotland. This document established the United Kingdom of Great Britain (also called Britain).

The 1700s

Queen Anne died in 1714, and her cousins—the Protestant Hanoverians of Germany—inherited the British throne. Under the Hanoverian kings, Britain increased its trade and naval power through explorations, military victories, and favorable peace treaties. The nation now had authority over much of North America and the Caribbean islands. English merchants expanded commercial and slave markets in Asia, South America, India, and Africa.

Parliament's importance grew under the Hanoverian kings, who authorized their council of parliamentary ministers to run the country. Because of this arrangement, the role and duties of the chief minister expanded and led to the establishment of a prime minister and a cabinet. These new leaders enacted policies that fostered trade and that strengthened England's control of its colonies.

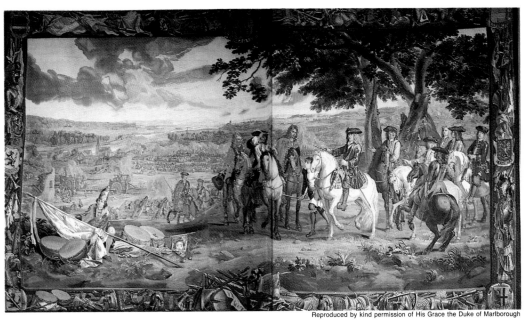

The left and right panels of a tapestry show the surrender of the French to the English after the Battle of Blenheim (now in West Germany) in 1704. Treaties after the battle gave England some of France's colonies in North America. The tapestry hangs in the Green Writing Room at Blenheim Palace—the home in southern England of the dukes of Marlborough. The first duke commanded the English forces at the Battle of Blenheim and commissioned the tapestry to commemorate the victory.

French and British soldiers engaged in hand-to-hand combat during the Battle of Waterloo in 1815. It was the decisive fight of Britain's wars against the French general Napoleon Bonaparte and established Britain as the most powerful European nation.

The United Kingdom lost some of its North American land in the late 1700s, when 13 of its colonies revolted to form the United States of America. Nevertheless, English merchants began to buy U.S. cotton in large quantities. In time, new weaving machines and power looms transformed the cloth industry and helped the cotton trade to grow. Improved yarn and thread supplied these manufacturing endeavors, which were located in central and northwestern England.

During this period, the English population increased. Many people moved to the emerging industrial cities—particularly Birmingham, Leeds, Manchester, and Liverpool. These cities had easy access to waterways and ports. Nearby deposits of coal powered new, steam-driven factories. Stocks of iron ore provided metal to build machines and equipment.

The increase in manufactured goods led to improvements in transportation. Crews of workers smoothed roads—some of which had existed for centuries—and built canals to connect rivers and ports. In time, railway lines crisscrossed England. These innovations were part of a transformation—known as the Industrial Revolution—that was taking place throughout Britain.

Effects of the Industrial Revolution

By the early 1800s, England had shifted its economic emphasis from farming to industry and trade. The Bank of England in London became the center of international money lending, and English investors funded ventures on six continents. As a result of these changes, English society became strictly layered into upper, middle and working classes.

During this period, Britain fought against Napoleon Bonaparte's French troops to protect Britain's markets and to remain in control of commercial sea-lanes. Military victories over Napoleon at Cape Trafalgar (near Spain) in 1805 and at Waterloo (in Belgium) in 1815 established Britain as the strongest nation in the world.

Photo by Mansell Collection

In the 1800s, England's industries expanded and improved, causing towns such as Sheffield, located in northern England, to grow in population and importance. Sheffield's factories produced high-quality steel, silver-plated items, and other metal goods.

Independent Picture Service

Much of England's vast industrial output was shipped to British colonies around the world. Here, workers unload barrels in Calcutta, a major port in northeastern India.

31

Despite England's prosperity—which generally benefited the upper and middle classes—the standard of living for most English people was poor. Conditions in the factories and cities were often harsh, and wages were low. Workers had little education, could not vote, and lived in poverty and filth. Health care was inadequate, and young children labored long hours in dangerous work environments.

By the 1830s, these concerns had attracted the attention of Parliament. It passed laws that regulated factory conditions and limited work hours for children. Other legislation legalized trade unions and extended the right to vote to men of the middle class. Parliament revised the ancient law code to eliminate unfair punishments, and it outlawed slavery in all British colonies.

Parliament itself underwent reform. For centuries, the great landowning families had controlled most seats in the legislature. In 1832 members passed laws to bring parliamentary representation to growing population centers, such as Leeds, Birmingham, and Manchester, none of which had delegates. Sparsely populated places lost their representation.

THE VICTORIAN ERA

The Industrial Revolution reached its peak in the nineteenth century during the reign of Queen Victoria, who inherited the throne in 1837. In her name, Parliament promoted trade throughout the British Empire, which included India, Australia, New Zealand, Canada, and other colonies in Africa, Asia, and the Caribbean.

Yet, during this same period, England itself experienced uneven progress. English mines produced half of the world's iron, but food shortages endangered the lives of the country's people. England's trade exceeded that of all other nations, but its workers could not vote. This state of affairs led to another wave of reform.

A public health act improved some harsh features of the workers' lives. Political

Courtesy of British Tourist Authority

The Houses of Parliament occupy a former royal palace on the Thames River in London. A disastrous fire in 1834 completely destroyed the buildings. At about the same time as reconstruction began, Parliament enacted reforms that enlarged its membership. In recent years, the exterior of the buildings—including the clock tower of Big Ben *(right)* —have been cleaned of decades of urban grime.

Independent Picture Service

Additional parliamentary changes in the 1800s were aimed at improving the lives of city dwellers, such as this family of vendors huddled together on a London street.

shifts caused the Liberal and Conservative parties to emerge from the old Whigs and Tories. William Gladstone headed the Liberals, and Benjamin Disraeli led the Conservatives. These two prime ministers took turns in holding the top governmental position between 1868 and 1885. They sponsored legislation that expanded voting rights to workers and that set up a national educational system. Reforms under later prime ministers brought some financial help to retired people and to ill or unemployed laborers.

In time, the reforms fostered the founding of the Labour party, which represented the interests of the workers. All classes of English society now had some political power, although it was still unevenly distributed. On the international scene, Britain used its commercial and naval supremacy to shape events in Europe. By entering into complex military alliances, British governments avoided major wars in the second half of the nineteenth century.

The Early 1900s

By the time of Queen Victoria's death in 1901, other nations—notably Germany and the United States—rivaled Britain's domination of manufacturing and of iron and steel production. By 1914 Germany, with a growing navy and industrial power, became the UK's main competitor for colonies, markets, and influence. In that year, Austria—Germany's ally—attacked Serbia in eastern Europe. Because of nineteenth-century alliances, this move brought Britain and its allies, France and Russia, into World War I. The allied forces fought against Germany, Austria, and Turkey.

Millions of Englishmen from every class and profession enlisted or were drafted to fight in France, Belgium, and the Middle East. Counties throughout England supplied regiments for the conflict, which at first had popular support. In their determination to help with the war effort, some Englishwomen took over jobs in factories, and others went overseas as nurses. Large estates were turned into recovery hospitals for wounded soldiers.

Public backing of the war declined, however, as the fighting dragged on and as thousands of young men died in unsuccessful campaigns. When World War I finally ended in 1918, Britain had lost more than 800,000 people.

Under the care of skilled nurses, soldiers wounded in World War I (1914–1918) recover at a hospital in France that was sponsored by the Duchess of Westminster. Many wealthy English people also allowed their large estates to be converted to hospitals to help the war effort.

Photo by Imperial War Museum

33

The global war changed English society. The class distinctions so strongly etched under Queen Victoria blurred in the post-war period under her grandson George V. Englishwomen strove to retain the independence they had won in the war years and gained the right to vote in 1918. The Labour party edged out the Liberal party, and power seesawed between Labour and Conservative governments. Farmers and factory workers—who had fought alongside landowners and factory managers—expected to share in the prosperity of peacetime.

These expectations were largely unmet because England's factories and farms suffered hardships during a severe, worldwide economic depression in the 1930s. Governments under both Labour and Conservative leaders tried to deal with three million unemployed workers, with shrinking markets, and with restless colonies. In addition to these difficulties, Germany—the loser in World War I—was again increasing its military, naval, and commercial power.

World War II and Its Aftermath

Some of the same issues that spurred English troops into action in 1914 resurfaced in the late 1930s. This time, however, the British government was less willing to get involved in an international conflict. Domestic affairs dominated the decisions of the Conservative prime minister, Neville Chamberlain.

Nevertheless, in September 1939, when Germany invaded Britain's ally Poland, Chamberlain reluctantly declared war. Soon afterward, he resigned his post, and Winston Churchill headed a coalition (mixed) cabinet composed of Liberals, Labourites, and Conservatives. World War II pitted the United Kingdom and its allies—the Soviet Union, the United States, and France—against Germany, Italy, and Japan.

Photo by Imperial War Museum

During World War II (1939–1945), Englishwomen made weapons, aircraft, and machinery in factories throughout the country.

Photo by Imperial War Museum

In Coventry—a city in central England —people pick through the rubble of Coventry Cathedral *(right)*, a fourteenth-century church destroyed in 1940. A modern cathedral replaced the ancient structure, which was made into a war memorial. Along with his aides, Prime Minister Winston Churchill *(below left, with walking stick)* examines bomb damage in London.

Photo by Imperial War Museum

In 1940 the German air force attacked the English coast and major cities. Daily bombings damaged railways, port facilities, factories, and housing in London, Coventry, Liverpool, Hull, Bristol, and Plymouth. Rationing of food and goods became a part of everyday life in England, as German submarines sank ships carrying tons of supplies to the island from overseas. Again, the determination of English people to support the war effort was strong. The Germans never invaded, and by 1943 the tide of war had turned in favor of the Allies. By 1945 the war was over. Much of urban England lay in ruins, and the country was deeply in debt.

After the war, a Labour government under Clement Attlee addressed the problems of destroyed factories, fewer markets, and lack of money. With loans from the United States, Britain began to rebuild its ruined economy. Attlee's government also enacted a program of nationalization. It transferred ownership of the coal, steel, railway, and other industries from private hands to the state. Even the Bank of England came under state control.

Also high on the list of Labour goals was a broad range of social legislation. Members of Parliament passed laws that provided national insurance for retired and unemployed people. The new National Health Service made almost every medical treatment available at little cost to patients.

The economy grew stronger in the 1950s and 1960s under a succession of Conservative governments that served in the name of the new queen, Elizabeth II. During these years, jobs were plentiful and wages were good. As a result, many English people could afford to own their homes and to furnish them with refrigerators and television sets. English people of all classes had access to a variety of

During the 1950s and 1960s, England welcomed many newcomers from other parts of the world. These young women—wearing clothes that were fashionable at the time—chat in the King's Road, the main thoroughfare through a London district called Chelsea.

In the early 1970s, striking workers carried signs protesting economic policies that restricted their wages. Strikes continued to occur throughout the decade, eventually toppling the government of the ruling Labour party.

leisure activities and could afford to take their vacations on the European mainland. New universities were built, and students had access to a greater number of scholarships than in previous decades. In search of a better standard of living, thousands of people from Britain's colonies immigrated to England.

ECONOMIC DECLINE

In the mid-1960s and 1970s, England felt the economic strains of fast recovery from wartime ruin. New social programs added to the financial burden. Britain decreased its international commitments by recalling its naval forces from Asia and by agreeing to self-rule for many of its colonies.

At home, unemployment rose as Britain's international markets shrank. The cost of living increased dramatically, and

members of trade unions staged dozens of strikes between 1972 and 1979 to get higher pay. Successive Labour governments tried to handle these problems. For instance, the United Kingdom joined the European Community (EC) in 1973, a move that opened some markets on the mainland to English goods. Investors developed newly discovered North Sea oil resources, which decreased the amount of money spent on imported oil.

Despite these efforts, the combination of high unemployment, rising inflation, and frequent strikes weakened the Labour government. The ruling party was also divided by the issue of nuclear disarmament—that is, ridding the nation of nuclear weapons. Some members of the Labour party wanted to make nuclear disarmament government policy. These factors helped to topple the Labour administration in 1979.

In 1981 – after two years of Conservative (Tory) rule – unemployed laborers and their families participated in the "People's March for Jobs." Organized by trade unions, the march aimed to weaken the Conservative government and to highlight the issue of rising unemployment.

An overturned car lies in front of the ruins of a looted store in Brixton, a low-income district in London. The damage occurred during riots in 1985.

Recent Events

Voters chose the Conservative party, headed by Margaret Thatcher, to succeed Labour. She became the first woman to serve as prime minister of Great Britain. Thatcher's goals included returning many of the nationalized industries to private ownership and decreasing the power of the trade unions. She also wanted to cut government spending on social services. Although her policies lowered inflation, unemployment continued to rise and strikes still occurred.

In 1982 English people were momentarily distracted from their economic woes by Britain's involvement in a war against Argentina. The conflict was over ownership of the Falklands, a small group of islands near South America that Britain and Argentina both claimed. A task force of 10,000 troops defeated the Argentines, and the Falklands war gave the prime minister a popularity boost.

Thatcher chose the moment to call a national election, and her party was returned to power in 1983 with a large majority. Another general election in 1987 gave Thatcher a rare third term in office. Helping her to win these victories was a lack of unity within the Labour party and the formation by dissatisfied Labourites of a fourth political group, the Social Democratic party.

The Thatcher government continued to pursue its economic plans. It called for less governmental spending and for the sale of nationalized industries to private corporations. By 1988 inflation and unemployment had risen, however, and support for the Conservatives was weakening.

As a result, Labour candidates did well in the 1989 elections to the European

The heir to the British throne is Charles, Prince of Wales. He and his wife, Diana, have two sons. Well-known symbols of national unity, Charles and his family work to promote British industries, products, and charities through public appearances. The prince's income—like that of his mother, the queen—comes from estates he and she each own throughout the kingdom. Other members of the royal family receive allowances that Parliament approves.

Courtesy of British Embassy

Parliament—the legislative arm of the EC—to which each member-country sends delegates. By 1992 the members of the EC will have eliminated all trade barriers among themselves, forming a single market. In so doing, England will become part of a combined trading bloc of 320 million consumers.

Despite this important move, English people have become reluctant Europeans. They continue to regard themselves as separate from the continent and take pride in England's long history and strong culture. In addition, most English people maintain ties with the region of their birth, whether it be Devon, the Midlands, or Yorkshire.

Many people feel that England itself is becoming split into two separate parts—southern and northern England. A Conservative stronghold, southern England has prospered during the Thatcher years. The north, on the other hand, has experienced growing unemployment and economic decline, and the large cities remain strongly pro-Labour. Much of England's future well-being will depend on its place among European nations and on the country's answers to ongoing economic and social questions.

Government

The United Kingdom has no written constitution. Instead, various parliamentary acts and common laws—some dating from Anglo-Saxon times—form the basis of government. Although symbolically headed by a monarch, the nation is governed by Parliament and by a cabinet made up of ministers who are also members of Parliament (MPs). The prime minister is the nation's most powerful political figure.

The British legislature has two parts. The democratically elected House of Commons is stronger than the hereditary House of Lords. The Commons has members from England, Scotland, Wales, and Northern Ireland. In 1990 the House of Commons had 523 MPs for England, out of a total of 650 delegates. MPs retain their seats for the life of the Parliament to which they are elected. By law, Parliaments may not sit for more than five years at a time. General elections may be held at shorter intervals.

The members of the House of Lords, who neither receive a salary nor seek election, hold office because of their aristocratic, honorary, or religious titles. The Lords cannot prevent a bill passed by the Commons from becoming law, but the members can delay certain legislation for up to one year. The House of Lords can also offer amendments to proposed laws, returning their ideas to the Commons for a final vote.

England's judicial system is based on parliamentary legislation and common law. Serious offenses are tried before the Crown Court, which consists of a judge and a jury. Magistrate courts, which justices of the peace operate, and county courts hear less serious cases. A decision by a magistrate court can be appealed to the Crown Court or the High Court. At the top of the judicial system are nine judges from the House of Lords, who deal with appeals from lower courts.

England's local government is in the hands of 39 nonmetropolitan counties and 7 metropolitan areas. One metropolitan area—Greater London—is divided into 32 boroughs plus the City of London. The counties, the metropolitan district councils, and London's borough councils have responsibility for education, public services, and roads.

Courtesy of British Information Service

Britain's most important national legislation comes out of the House of Commons. Members of the ruling party, who form the government, sit to the right of the speaker *(seated center)*. The front bench holds the heads of departments and ministries. To the speaker's left sit members of opposition parties. Here, Neil Kinnock *(standing center at the table)*—the leader of the Labour party—makes a point during a debate in 1989. By tradition, members addressing the Commons may not step over the rust-colored stripes on the carpet. The distance from one side of the carpet to the other is supposed to be the length of two drawn swords.

Photo by Kay Shaw Photography

English families are typically small in size, with a statistical average of 1.8 children per woman of child-bearing age. Inhabitants of England have a higher income per person than do the people of Wales, Scotland, and Northern Ireland—the other countries that make up the United Kingdom. England also has the lowest unemployment rate and the highest population density in the nation.

3) The People

Most of the United Kingdom's citizens live in England. In 1990 the country had 47 million inhabitants out of a total of 57 million British people. About 90 percent of the English population are urban dwellers. Because of the country's small land area, England's population density is high —about 940 people per square mile. Nevertheless, many regions—the Lake District in Cumbria and the moors in Devon, for example—are sparsely settled.

Ethnic Mixture

Most English people are descendants of various European groups—including Celts, Romans, Anglo-Saxons, Danes, and Normans—that invaded and settled in the country. England still contains reminders of their presence, ranging from Celtic chalk figures to Norman cathedrals.

The two world wars blurred the wealth-related distinctions that had arisen among English people in the 1700s and 1800s. Social divisions still exist, but they are not as strict as they were. For example, every prime minister since 1964 has come from the middle or working class. In addition, by adopting their own fashions and style of language, young English people have removed some of the class differences that once were marked by clothing and speech.

Some young English people express their individual tastes and identities in their clothing and hairstyles.

Throughout the twentieth century, people from Europe, India, Pakistan, Hong Kong, and the Caribbean immigrated to England. Many arrived as refugees, while others came in search of a better life from former colonies. In 1990 these immigrants numbered two million. They usually live in the inner cities, which suffer from unemployment. These minority groups often experience discrimination while trying to get housing and jobs.

A new factor of English life has been urban unrest, much of it rooted in ethnic differences. In London, Liverpool, Bristol, and Birmingham, riots have occurred in black and Asian neighborhoods. Many people believe that the unrest is related to economic problems, such as unemployment, and to poor relations between police and residents. The 1987 general election brought the first Asian and black MPs into the legislature, and ethnic self-help programs operate within minority communities.

Members of an Indian family in London retain ties to their homeland's customs by eating a traditional meal together in their living room.

Health and Welfare

Since 1945, England has been part of a welfare state—that is, a nation where the government provides for the well-being of all of its citizens. A major part of this effort is the National Health Service, which offers most medical services at minimal cost to patients. This comprehensive program has brought many diseases under control. The National Health Service has

also helped to lower the number of English infants who die within the first year of life. At 9 deaths per 1,000 live births, the infant mortality rate is among the best in the world. The average life expectancy for an English person is 74. The major health threats in England are heart disease, cancer, and stroke.

In the 1980s, concern grew over the spread of acquired immune deficiency syn-

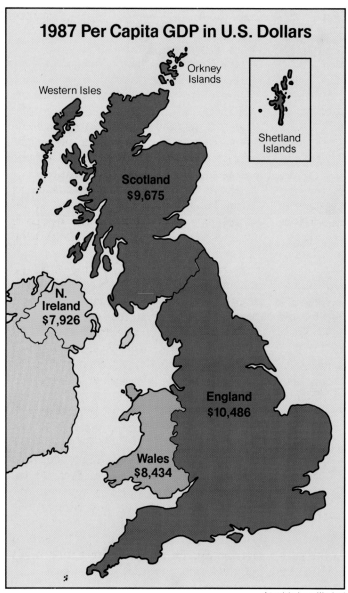

1987 Per Capita GDP in U.S. Dollars

Orkney Islands

Western Isles

Shetland Islands

Scotland $9,675

N. Ireland $7,926

England $10,486

Wales $8,434

Artwork by Laura Westlund

This map compares the average wealth per person—calculated by gross domestic product (GDP) per capita—for the four countries that make up the United Kingdom. The GDP is the value of all goods and services produced within the borders of each country in a year. To arrive at the GDP per capita, each country's total GDP is divided by its population. The resulting dollar amounts indicate one measure of the quality of life in Britain. The overall GDP figure for the United Kingdom is $10,239, but England's amount is slightly higher because of its wide variety of economic activities. Free medical care and other welfare services also give most English people a good standard of living. (Data taken from *Britain 1990*, prepared by the Central Office of Information.)

Uniformed schoolgirls pass in front of a petrol (gas) station in the Cotswolds—a range of hills in west central England.

drome (AIDS) in the United Kingdom. The government devoted funds to AIDS education and to careful screening of blood donations. Money was also set aside to treat drug users, who have a greater chance than most people of catching AIDS.

Another aspect of the welfare state is the social security system, which provides funds to the elderly, the sick, the disabled, the unemployed, and widows. Social security expenses have risen dramatically in recent years because of high unemployment. Some English people, particularly youth from large urban centers, live off their welfare checks for long periods—a situation called "being on the dole."

Women have made significant strides in England since World War I, when they gained the right to vote. This change began the long effort to remove all sexual discrimination at the political, legal, and professional levels. Since 1945, women have had a strong role in the work force, although wages still tend to be lower for women than they are for men.

Education

In England, all children between the ages of 5 and 16 must attend school. About 99 percent of the population can read and write. Most children go to schools that the government funds. Some of these schools have religious ties—mainly with the Church of England or the Roman Catholic Church. A small number of students attend elite, private institutions, such as Eton College, Harrow, and Charterhouse. These institutions, which charge fees, have long been called "public," although they function as private schools.

Primary school lasts roughly until age 11, and secondary students complete their studies at age 16. Most secondary schools are comprehensives—that is, they provide a wide range of courses and do not distinguish between pupils according to ability. Postsecondary options for English students include technical, vocational, and academic training.

Among the most prestigious English universities are Oxford, founded in the 1100s, and Cambridge, established in the 1200s. Famous for their high academic standards, these two independent institutions are made up of many separate colleges. Since 1945, the government has founded other universities, including the Open University. This institution, which has no regular campus, offers its courses on television, on radio, on video cassettes, and through the mail.

Religion and Language

The Church of England (or Anglican Church) is the country's official religious institution. Until the mid-nineteenth century, people who were not members of the Church of England could not sit in Parliament and could not attend the colleges at Oxford or Cambridge. These religious restrictions no longer exist. Although millions of English people belong to the Church of England, many of them do not regularly attend services.

Other Protestant sects flourish in England and are called free churches because they are not tied to the state. These groups include the Methodist and the Baptist churches. Some sects developed under intense persecution when dissatisfied Anglicans broke away from the Church of England. Similarly, the Roman Catholic Church experienced discrimination in earlier centuries but now has full powers to establish schools and churches.

England contains one of Europe's largest Jewish congregations, numbering about 400,000. Many of the group's members came to England to escape persecution in Germany, the Soviet Union, and Eastern Europe earlier in the twentieth century. Jewish communities also run their own schools, as well as welfare agencies for Jewish people who are elderly or disabled.

As a result of recent immigrations, many English cities have large Sikh, Hindu, and Islamic congregations. Members of the Sikh and Hindu faiths generally have an Indian background, while the followers of Islam come mostly from Pakistan, Bangladesh, and the Middle East. These groups often support their own schools in an effort to preserve their religious heritage in England.

Although newcomers have brought many other languages to England, the country's official language is English. Rooted in the Germanic languages of the Anglo-Saxons, the English language is usually divided into three stages of development.

Independent Picture Service

The twelfth-century interior of Durham Cathedral *(above)* **contrasts sharply with the modern design of the new Coventry Cathedral, completed in 1962** *(below)*.

Independent Picture Service

BRITISH	AMERICAN
biro	ballpoint pen
bonnet	car hood
boot	car trunk
call box	phone booth
fringe	bangs
jumper	sweater
lift	elevator
lorry	trunk
nappy	baby's diaper
petrol	gasoline
plimsoles	tennis shoes
pram	baby carriage
slide	barrette
sweet	piece of candy
torch	flashlight
wireless	radio

Although people in both England and the United States speak English, there are variations in some common terms. This list shows a few everyday words that are different in British and American English but that have the same meaning.

In a corner of St. Paul's Cathedral in London stands "Madonna and Child," a sculpture by the twentieth-century, Yorkshire-born artist Henry Moore. His smooth, scooped-out figures suggest a baby resting in the arms of its mother.

Old English—used in the earliest written records, including *The Anglo-Saxon Chronicle*—dates to about 1100. Middle English, which shows some Norman-French influence, was common from 1100 to the late 1400s. Since then, people have spoken modern English, which was used in a famous seventeenth-century translation of the Bible. Known as the King James Version (after King James I), this translation influenced many English writers and composers.

Although all English people speak English, dialects exist in various parts of the country. For example, people from Liverpool speak a variation called scouse, and the residents of Newcastle upon Tyne use Geordie. Some Londoners speak the cockney dialect. To English-speakers outside these areas, the special dialects can be hard to understand. Despite decades of radio and television broadcasts—in which the most accepted style of English is used—regional speech differences often reinforce class distinctions.

Art and Music

English architects and painters have been important members of the country's artistic community. During the 1600s, Christopher Wren and Inigo Jones designed and reshaped buildings in London and in many other parts of England. These two architects reintroduced the classical style, which features variations on ancient Greek and Roman structures.

In the 1700s, artists such as William Hogarth and Thomas Rowlandson poked fun at English society through their caricatures. Formal portrait painters followed, including Joshua Reynolds and Thomas Gainsborough. Landscape artists, such as John Constable and J. M. W. Turner, produced images of the English countryside in the 1800s. During these centuries, fine furniture designs from Thomas Chippendale and Thomas Sheraton changed the interior decor of many houses. At the same time, porcelain from the china factories of Josiah Wedgwood and Herbert Minton in Stoke-on-Trent appeared on English tables.

The twentieth century has brought forth a variety of artistic forms. The Yorkshire-born sculptors Henry Moore and Barbara Hepworth favored smooth, rounded shapes in their works of wood and stone. Francis Bacon's paintings depict horrifying events, while the art of David Hockney presents bold, familiar images.

Among important early English composers are William Byrd and Henry Purcell. Byrd, who wrote in the late 1500s and early 1600s, based some of his composi-

tions on traditional English folk music. Purcell composed pieces for harpsichord, organ, and voice in the late seventeenth century. In the 1700s, under the Hanoverian kings, the German-born composer George Frideric Handel wrote music for royal occasions as well as for Anglican services. Between 1875 and 1896, W. S. Gilbert and Arthur Sullivan produced 14 operettas, most of which have gained worldwide popularity. Edward Elgar and Ralph Vaughan Williams are well-known English composers from the early 1900s.

In the 1960s, England became the center of a revolution in popular music begun by the Beatles, who came out of Liverpool in

Courtesy of James E. Laib

The organ at the abbey church in Bath has 4,242 pipes. The large instrument is used both for religious services and for nonreligious concerts.

In the early 1960s, four young men from Liverpool – *(from left)* Ringo Starr, George Harrison, John Lennon, and Paul McCartney – transformed rock-and-roll music. Their group, known as the Beatles, made many hit records and several films before disbanding in 1970. Many other musicians in England patterned themselves after the Beatles.

the early part of the decade. They were followed by many other English rock performers, including the Rolling Stones, The Who, Eric Clapton, and David Bowie.

More recent rock bands, such as Dire Straits and The Cure, have mixed new ideas with traditional rock-and-roll sounds.

Literature

Several of England's earliest authors—such as The Venerable Bede, who compiled *The Ecclesiastical* (Church) *History of the English People*—composed in Latin. The first person to achieve lasting distinction in English, however, was Geoffrey Chaucer, who wrote *The Canterbury Tales* in the 1300s. In this work, pilgrims entertain each other with wild and funny stories while traveling to the shrine of Thomas Becket in Canterbury.

William Shakespeare, an outstanding English literary figure of the 1500s, is considered one of the greatest poets and

One of the characters in Geoffrey Chaucer's *The Canterbury Tales* is the wife of Bath. To entertain her fellow pilgrims, she tells the story of a knight whose quest is to find out what women desire most in life.

47

The Frankenstein monster—one of the world's most famous scary characters—was the creation of the English writer Mary Shelley. Married in 1816 to the poet Percy Bysshe Shelley, she got the idea for her horror story while they were on vacation in Italy.

English actors have performed the plays of William Shakespeare for many centuries. Here, the late Laurence Olivier—among England's greatest classical actors—does a scene from *Hamlet*, in which he played the title role.

playwrights of all time. He created tragic, comic, and historic plays—including *Hamlet, As You Like It,* and *Henry V*—which are still performed throughout the world. In the 1600s, the English poets John Donne and John Milton used religious symbols to comment on love and society. The spicy diary of Samuel Pepys provides a vivid, eyewitness account of the Great Fire of London, which raged through the capital in 1666.

The 1700s brought the poetry and critical essays of Alexander Pope, as well as Daniel Defoe's *Robinson Crusoe.* Defoe's writing style soon led to the development of the novel, a literary format used by Henry Fielding for his book *Tom Jones.* The late 1700s and early 1800s are noted for poets— such as William Blake, William Wordsworth, and Samuel Taylor Coleridge—

whose verse reflects a love of nature. Lord Byron, John Keats, and Percy Bysshe Shelley wrote in the Romantic style, which uses passionate language and lush imagery. At the same time, Mary Shelley wrote the popular science-fiction story *Frankenstein.*

Among many prominent nineteenth-century novelists were Jane Austen, Charlotte Brontë, and Charles Dickens. In his novels, such as *Oliver Twist,* Dickens revealed the abuses of Victorian England. His writings contributed to many of the social reforms that later took place. Thomas Hardy wrote of rural life in his native Dorset, which he called Wessex.

In the early twentieth century, the works of E. M. Forster, Virginia Woolf, H. G. Wells, Evelyn Waugh, and D. H. Lawrence examined colonial and social issues. The mystery novels of Dorothy L. Sayers and Agatha Christie also originated in England at this time. The experiences of both world wars produced forceful poets, such as Siegfried Sassoon and Wilfred Owen, and writers, such as Graham Greene and John Osborne.

In recent years, English playwrights have brought new ideas to the stage. Harold Pinter's plays show ordinary people in tense situations, and Tom Stoppard's works contain fast-paced verbal exchanges and complex plots. The novelists John Le Carré and P. D. James have produced sophisticated thrillers, while Barbara Pym uses a calm, gentle style to describe English life.

Sports and Recreation

Since 1945, English people increasingly have had time to enjoy a wide variety of athletic activities. The country's most popular sport is football (soccer), which city and regional teams play professionally as members of the Football Association of England. In the 1980s, violence by English fans at national and international football matches caused widespread concern.

Cricket—a bat-and-ball game that pits two 11-member teams against one another —is played in villages and schools throughout the country. A cricket team representing England competes against groups from many former British colonies in annual matches.

Sports fans also enjoy watching rugby, a fast-moving game that inspired U.S. football. Snooker—a type of pool—and bowls (a form of bowling played on a lawn) are very popular. Tennis, golf, badminton, and fishing also have strong followings. English athletes have excelled in Olympic competition, recently winning medals in figure skating and track events.

Many English people use their leisure time to ride horses and to walk in the countryside. National parks and county preserves protect certain parts of England from industrial development. Closer to home, English people enjoy tending their gardens, which can range in size from a small patch to many acres.

Courtesy of Rugby Advertiser

Wearing padded gloves and leg shields, a batsman *(above)* swats at an oncoming cricket ball. Standing behind him is the wicket keeper, who will try to eliminate the batsman by knocking two thin pieces of wood off the wicket *(left, behind the batsman)* when the batsman is out of position. In another popular sport *(right)*, football (soccer) players jostle each other to gain control of the ball.

Courtesy of Rugby Advertiser

49

Food

Once based on what was readily available, English foods have developed as regional specialties. Cornish pasties—pastry shells filled with meat and potatoes—were lunches for men who worked in the tin mines of Cornwall. Sheep that grazed on northern moors provided lamb for Lancashire hot pots (lamb stews). Since their country is nearly surrounded by water, the English favor fish, such as sole from Dover and herrings from Great Yarmouth.

Certain favorite dishes appear on the menus of English restaurants and public houses (pubs). These specialties include shepherd's pie (hamburger topped with mashed potatoes) and Yorkshire pudding. This rib-sticking batter is baked in the roasting pan with roast beef. Among stan-dard pub fare are bangers and mash (sausages and mashed potatoes) and bubble and squeak (leftover meat and cabbage fried in beef drippings). Pubs also serve locally brewed beer and cider.

A well-established English custom, drinking tea and eating cakes at teatime—about 4:00 P.M.—occurs in urban businesses as well as rural kitchens. Clotted cream—a thick, sticky spread used with jam on scones (biscuits)—is served at special teas. With its emphasis on cattle raising, England makes a wide variety of other milk-based products. English cheeses remain tied by tradition to the regions that first produced them. For example, farmhouse Cheddar is still made in the southwest, and blue Stilton comes only from a few counties in central England.

Courtesy of Bob Wolfe

Shepherd's pie consists of whipped potatoes spread over a mixture of hamburger and spices.

Up-to-date technology – including assembly-line robots – is a major feature of English factories, which must compete against U.S., Japanese, and European manufacturers.

4) The Economy

One of the world's major manufacturers, England became the hub of a great commercial and political empire in the mid-nineteenth century. In modern times, England's markets have shrunk because of competition from other industrialized countries. Nevertheless, Britain remains among the top 10 trading nations in the world.

In 1973 Britain joined the European Community (EC), and prices for English goods became subject to EC rules. Regional and national concerns have hampered previous efforts to unite the EC members into a single trading bloc, but this project is now well under way. The first step—

removing all trade barriers between EC nations—should be completed by 1992. This change will transform Western Europe into a united marketplace, rivaling U.S. and Japanese buying power.

Manufacturing and Trade

Despite its loss of some markets, England remains dependent on manufacturing and trade for its income. Industrial complexes dot the English countryside. They were once constructed near plentiful sources of fuel (mainly coal) but now are concentrated in the Midlands and the south. Since northern England was the country's key

Since the 1700s, the pottery factories in Stoke-on-Trent have produced internationally famous ceramics. A craftsperson applies decorations by hand to a piece of jasparware. This method of ornamenting pottery has changed little since the 1800s because the technique is ideal for creating lasting detail.

Courtesy of Wedgwood

A trade-dependent country, England has many large and small ports. Here, container-laden vehicles line up beneath giant cranes at Harwich, an eastern harbor that handles shipments from the European mainland.

Independent Picture Service

industrial area in the 1800s, this southward shift has hurt local businesses and has eliminated jobs in the north.

English factories produce transportation equipment, such as locomotives, ships, cars, and aircraft. Consumer goods—including textiles, pottery, plastics, electronic equipment, processed foods, and alcoholic beverages—are also made. Firms that manufacture iron and steel products are concentrated in northeastern England, where stocks of iron and steel are located.

Cars come from Birmingham, Dagenham, Coventry, and Liverpool. Plants in northern England make textiles, and companies in Birmingham, Manchester, and Leeds produce sophisticated electronic equipment.

England depends on foreign trade to sell its large manufacturing inventory. Income from the trade buys the raw materials that English factories need to make more products. As a result of its commercial dependence, the English economy rises and falls with changes in world markets. The EC and the United States buy most of England's exports, which include chemicals, petroleum, and transportation equipment. The chief imports are food—particularly tea and citrus fruits, which do not grow well in England—and raw materials.

Agriculture and Fishing

England produces about 60 percent of the food it needs on small farms that employ

Courtesy of Richard Rodgers

less than 2 percent of the population. The remainder of the country's food is imported. England's climate is appropriate for cultivating only a limited number of crops but is well suited to growing rich pastureland. The raising of livestock, therefore, dominates the agricultural sector.

Most dairy cattle are raised in the west, where heavy rains stimulate the growth of nutritious grasses. Sheep are found most often in northern and southwestern England, where they feed on the grasslands of the moors. A modern and efficient business, crop farming is concentrated in the rich soils of northern England and the Fens, where potatoes and vegetables are common products. Eastern and southern England produce fruits, sugar beets, and cereal grains such as wheat and barley.

England's irregular coastline offers many places for the fishing industry to flourish. In an average year, the country's fishermen haul in thousands of tons of seafood. Herring, cod, and whitefish dominate the catch, but shellfish and mackerel are also common.

The main fishing ports lie along England's eastern coast at Lowestoft, North Shields, Hull, and Grimsby. Commercial fishermen may drop their nets close to shore in search of shellfish or go out a bit farther to find whitefish and migrating herring.

At a dairy farm in Dorset *(above)*, Friesian cows have their afternoon milking. The dairyman *(standing)* attaches equipment to the cows' teats as the animals stand in separate stalls. Once a month, a milk recorder *(kneeling)* from the Ministry of Agriculture checks the milk yields of each cow. Using a small tractor *(right)*, a farmer overturns his field in neat rows. Because of modern agricultural methods, England's farmland produces very high crop volumes.

Independent Picture Service

Fishing vessels lie ready to venture into the English Channel at Plymouth—a shipping and fishing hub in southwestern England.

Photo by Robert W. Nelson

Some firms hire people to explore the Atlantic Ocean and the North Sea, where they fish for months at a time. The catches are frozen on board large fishing vessels.

Mining and Energy

Huge deposits of iron (for building equipment) and coal (for fuel) made England the center of the nineteenth-century Industrial Revolution. Years of mining have largely exhausted England's stocks of iron ore, but the land still contains substantial supplies of coal. About 80 percent of Britain's coal is located in northern and central England. Although deposits are still being worked, many coal pits have closed since 1970, as supplies disappear and as other fuels replace coal.

Among these other fuels are oil and natural gas—both discovered in the North Sea, off England's eastern coast. As a result of these finds, England became an international supplier of fossil fuels—a resource the country had previously imported. This change improved England's economic outlook, since the government spent less money on foreign petroleum and generated income from the sale of North Sea oil.

Wicker devices for snaring fish line the quay (landing area) of Hugh Town, a fishing site in the Scilly Isles.

A natural gas terminal at Easington, North Yorkshire, receives products from the North Sea.

These miners are wearing the dust and grime that come from chipping and carving the coalface. Equipment does much of the heaviest labor in underground mines.

Courtesy of British Coal Corporation

In the late 1980s, the United Kingdom produced about 900 million barrels of oil each year, making the nation one of the top 10 oil producers in the world. The main

North Sea oil fields lie off Scotland's eastern coast, but other finds are located about 200 miles from northeastern England. Pipelines carry the crude oil to coastal

Photo by Christabel D. Grant

Near Stafford in western England, a strip mine is scored with gouges made to extract the coal that lies near the earth's surface.

Courtesy of Minneapolis Public Library and Information Center

An abandoned tin mine in Cornwall is a reminder of the region's former importance as a metal producer. England's deposits of tin are virtually exhausted.

Courtesy of Minneapolis Public Library and Information Center

The tall cones of a nuclear power station rise above the land in northern England. Great Britain uses nuclear-generated electricity to supply more than 18 percent of its energy needs.

terminals, and major refineries exist near Middlesbrough in the northeast and near London in southeastern England.

Natural gas deposits lie in the North Sea off the eastern coast. Pipelines bring the gas to coastal terminals, and the product is then transported inland. In the late 1980s, Britain produced enough natural gas to meet three-fourths of its gas needs. Nuclear reactors, hydropower, and coal- and oil-burning plants supplied the rest of the nation's energy.

Transportation and Tourism

England's well-established transportation system fostered the growth of mining and manufacturing ventures. The country maintains more than 200,000 miles of roads. Many of the main routes—such as the Fosse Way and Watling Street—are ancient Roman thoroughfares. These have now been upgraded to modern highways and link large sections of the country. Since the 1950s, motorways (freeways) and shorter highways have made travel throughout England easy and fast. Two out of three English people own cars, and the motorways between London and other large cities are crowded at peak times.

Supplementing the road system is a sophisticated railway network that connects all parts of the country. Workers laid most of the track in the nineteenth century, but

57

Motorways provide fast, overland connections throughout the United Kingdom, but especially in England. In British-made cars, the steering wheel is on the right side, and on a two-way street motorists drive in the left lane. (In most other nations, the steering wheel is on the left, and drivers use the right lane.)

Courtesy of Wayland (Publishers) Limited

London's tube speeds along track that lies both below and above the ground, depending on the location of the station. Ten lines that crisscross at many points can take riders nearly anywhere in the capital. This train is part of the Victoria Line, which runs through central London in a southwest-northeast direction.

Independent Picture Service

Courtesy of James E. Laib

Hovercrafts—vehicles supported on a cushion of air that is forced downward against the sea—cross the English Channel between Dover, England, and the French ports of Boulogne and Calais.

58

rail lines and trains have been frequently upgraded. Travelers can take comfortable, high-speed trains between cities and can use underground systems to complete trips within some large urban areas.

Traffic between the United Kingdom and France is often heavy. As a result, the governments of both nations conceived the idea of a cross-channel tunnel—nicknamed the Chunnel—to run beneath the English Channel. Begun in 1988, the Chunnel will offer a rail link with Europe when completed in the mid-1990s.

Oil exports and increases in European trade have fostered improvements in shipping facilities throughout England. The country's main cargo ports are at London, Grimsby, Hartlepool, and Felixstowe. Britain's merchant fleet uses these ports to carry English products to international

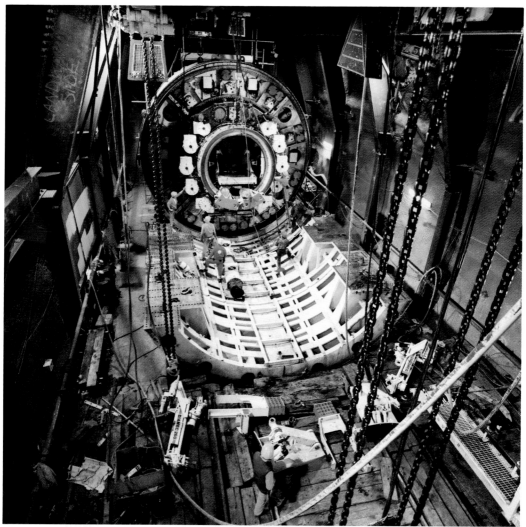

Photo by Q. A. Photo Library

Construction of a cross-channel tunnel—or Chunnel—began in the late 1980s. Designed to carry both passengers and freight to and from the mainland, the Chunnel consists of three tunnels—two for travel and one to provide a repair route. High-speed electric trains will be able to complete the trip from Folkstone (near Dover) to Coquelles (near Calais) in about 35 minutes. Due to be completed in the mid-1990s, the project has had financial and labor problems.

Courtesy of Gordon L. Levine

Many visitors from North America land at Terminal 3 of London's Heathrow Airport.

don. Heathrow is the hub of British Airways, the nation's largest airline, which flies the supersonic *Concorde*—the world's fastest commercial airplane. In recent years, the traffic at Gatwick and Stansted airports, which also lie within a short distance of the capital, has increased. Other major air terminals exist in Manchester, Luton, and Birmingham.

Every year, millions of foreign travelers arrive at England's airports and docks, making tourism a major source of national income. Many vacationers remain in London, enjoying its theaters, museums, and public celebrations involving the British royal family. Other tourists journey to Norman castles, eighteenth-century country homes, small village pubs, and areas of natural beauty that lie beyond the capital. About 60 percent of the visitors come from Western Europe, and about 20 percent originate in North America.

In the 1980s, roughly 12 million people a year visited Britain, which earned more than $5 billion from tourist activities.

destinations. In addition to cargo, terminals in Dover and Southampton accommodate substantial passenger traffic.

England contains several airports, the busiest of which is Heathrow, near Lon-

Independent Picture Service

For outdoor enthusiasts, Hadrian's Wall—located in the far north of England—is a favorite destination. Built by the Romans in the A.D. 120s, the barrier was designed to keep out Scottish raiders called Picts.

This long, half-timbered house near Stratford-upon-Avon is a popular tourist site. Shakespeare's mother—Mary Arden—lived here until her marriage. The sixteenth-century dwelling has been carefully preserved as part of the Shakespeare Birthplace Trust.

At Chester, an old market town near the Welsh border, morris dancers perform during a local festival. Morris dancing dates from the eleventh century, when soldiers from England engaged in crusades against armies made up of Arabs (called "Moors" by the Europeans). "Morris" is a variation on the word *Moorish,* and this male dance involves stamping and leaping while waving pieces of cloth and jingling bells.

Windsurfers and boats—as well as large passenger vessels—compete for space in Southampton, England's busy southern port.

The front of Harrod's—perhaps London's most famous department store—displays various royal coats of arms. The emblems signify that Harrod's has been appointed to supply certain goods to members of the royal family. Tourists, Londoners, and English visitors also frequent the food hall, clothing departments, and other specialty shops at Harrod's.

In addition to the foreign trade, many parts of England benefit from domestic tourism. With its pleasant climate, southwestern England attracts the largest number of British citizens, and the offshore Scilly Isles are a favorite destination. The beaches at Brighton and Blackpool and the shores of the Lake District draw English people in search of sunshine, which is sometimes hard to find in England.

The Future

In the 1990s, the policies of the EC will have a direct bearing on England's economic position. For example, the price of English goods will be tied to the cost of products made on the European mainland. Lower European taxes and relaxed labor laws may go a long way toward addressing England's income and unemployment problems.

Throughout their history, the English have adapted to changing circumstances. The English character, however, has remained rooted in its traditional culture. England's achievements in literature, science, architecture, and music have earned global attention. These features and the country's symbols of unity—including Parliament and the royal family—attract millions of visitors each year. Promoting economic stability, responding to events in Europe, and preserving England's identity are among the challenges of the coming decades.

Photo by Robert W. Nelson

As crowds watch, Queen Elizabeth II guides her horse through a military pageant known as Trooping the Colour. It takes place each June and commemorates the queen's official birthday.

Index

942
Eng

910546

England in pictures